PARTNERS IN EVANGELIZATION

Chinese American Catholics

Committee on Cultural Diversity in the Church
Subcommittee on Asian and Pacific Island Affairs

United States Conference of Catholic Bishops
Washington, DC

Partners in Evangelization: Chinese American Catholics was developed by the Subcommittee on Asian and Pacific Island Affairs of the United States Conference of Catholic Bishops (USCCB). It was reviewed by the Committee on Cultural Diversity in the Church, and it was approved by the Administrative Committee at its March 2021 meeting. It has been directed for publication by the undersigned.

Reverend Michael J.K. Fuller, S.Th.D.
General Secretary, USCCB

Cover image: *Our Lady of China* mosaic based on painting by John Lu Hung-Nien. © Basilica of the National Shrine of the Immaculate Conception, Washington, D.C. Photographer: Geraldine M. Rohling.

Quotes from Pope John Paul II and Pope Benedict, copyright © Libreria Editrice Vaticana (LEV), Vatican City State. Used with permission. All rights reserved.

Scripture excerpts used in this work are taken from the New American Bible, revised edition, copyright © 2010, 1991, 1986, 1970 Confraternity of Christian Doctrine, Inc., Washington, DC. All rights reserved

First Printing, October 2021

ISBN 978-1-60137-690-9

Copyright © 2021, United States Conference of Catholic Bishops, Washington, DC. All rights reserved.

Contents

Foreword 1
Introduction 3
1. History of Chinese American Catholics 5
   1.1 Cantonese-Speaking Chinese Catholics 6
   1.2 Mandarin-Speaking Chinese Catholics 9
   1.3 Fujianese-Speaking Chinese Catholics 11
2. Chinese Catholic Community in
Contemporary United States 12
   2.1 Chinese Catholic Communities in the
   United States Today 12
   2.2 Chinese Catholic Associations in the United States ... 13
   2.3 Chinese Catholic Customs and Practices 14
      2.3.1 Inculturation of the Gospel with Confucian Values;
      Matteo Ricci 14
      2.3.2 Marian Devotion 17
      2.3.3 Special Days on the Chinese Calendar 18
      2.3.4 Colors and Numbers in Chinese Culture 19
   2.4 Pastoral Considerations for Ministering to
   Chinese Americans 20
      2.4.1 Complexities of the Chinese Language 20
      2.4.2 Generational Differences and Pastoral Needs ... 22
3. Chinese American Catholic Community:
Opportunities and Future Directions 24
   3.1 Ministering to Chinese Immigrants 24
      3.1.1 Welcoming the Immigrant 25
      3.1.2 Separated Families, Remarriage, Interracial Marriage .. 25
      3.1.3 Ministering to Working Immigrants 25
   3.2 Vocations, Evangelization, and Ministry 26
      3.2.1 Vocations 26
      3.2.2 Indirect Missionary Work in China 27

    3.2.3 Evangelizing Chinese Students. 27
    3.2.4 Supporting the Church in China 29
   3.3 Chinese Catholics Enrich the Church in the
   United States 29
Conclusion. 31
   Figure 1. Map of Chinese Catholic
   Communities in the United States. 32
   Table 1. US Catholic Population, Race,
   Ethnicity, and Birthplace Estimates, 2013.. 33
   Table 2. Chinese Catholic Communities in the
   United States 34
   Table 3. Calendar of Key Chinese Festivals 37
   Table 4. Calendar of Chinese Liturgical Feasts 39
Bibliography 45

Foreword

PARTNERS IN EVANGELIZATION: CHINESE AMERICAN CATHOLICS

In 2018, the United States Conference of Catholic Bishops' statement *Encountering Christ in Harmony: A Pastoral Response to Our Asian and Pacific Island Brothers and Sisters* affirmed the need to "provide and continue to develop resources that are prepared for—and may stem from—Asian and Pacific Island communities."

The preceding US bishops' pastoral statement, *Asian and Pacific Presence: Harmony in Faith* (2001), recommended the development of a series of educational materials about Asian and Pacific Island Catholics in the United States. In 2011, to mark the tenth anniversary of the promulgation of *Harmony in Faith*, the Subcommittee on Asian and Pacific Island Affairs (SCAPA) encouraged the observance of the special anniversary and promoted the implementation of the vision of the pastoral statement in several ways, including the development of educational materials for publication about Asian and Pacific Island Catholics.

The SCAPA commissioned draft writers for a series of small books to foster knowledge of and awareness among clergy, ministers, and parishioners of the traditions and expressions of faith of Catholics of Asian and Pacific Island descent.

The Subcommittee is grateful to Carolyn Yeehan Ng, MTS, and Deacon Christopher J. Yeung, PhD, for their work on *Partners in Evangelization: Chinese American Catholics*. Ms. Ng is a catechetical leader in the Archdiocese of Washington and is also an ethnic ministry adviser to the SCAPA. Deacon Yeung presently serves as the delegate for the archbishop of Baltimore to western Maryland.

This small book sets out to provide readers with a general introduction to Chinese American Catholicism from historical, cultural, worship, and pastoral perspectives. This concise resource is replete with useful information that may be helpful for pastors and those involved in ministry to the Chinese Americans. It provides key insights into the cultural traits and faith perspectives that animate the religious life of Chinese Americans today.

Most Rev. Oscar A. Solis, D.D.
Bishop of Salt Lake City
Chairman of the Subcommittee on Asian and Pacific Island Affairs,
United States Conference of Catholic Bishops

Introduction

In June 2018, the United States Conference of Catholic Bishops (USCCB) approved the pastoral statement *Encountering Christ in Harmony: A Pastoral Response to Our Asian and Pacific Island Brothers and Sisters*. This document fulfilled a pastoral need, first described in their earlier 2001 document *Asian and Pacific Presence: Harmony in Faith*, to develop a national pastoral plan for Asian and Pacific Island (API) Catholics in the United States. The USCCB has written these documents "to assist diocesan and parish leaders and all the faithful in welcoming and integrating our Asian and Pacific Island brothers and sisters"[1] into the Catholic Church in the United States. Central to this task is for church leaders to recognize the rich and deep history of Catholicism among the diverse API cultures so that API Catholics are able to "share their experiences and gifts as well as to receive support from the wider Catholic Church in the United States."[2] When fully implemented, this initiative will go a long way towards achieving the vision of unity Jesus expressed in Gethsemane, "so that they may all be one, as you, Father, are in me and I in you, that they also may be in us, that the world may believe that you sent me" (Jn 17:21).

To assist diocesan and parish leaders in recognizing the richness of Catholic faith and heritage among API Catholics, the USCCB's Subcommittee on Asian and Pacific Island Affairs (SCAPA) commissioned a series of small books about each country's Catholics. This small book on Chinese Catholics in the United States is the fifth in this series, following previous books about Filipino Catholics (2020), Chamorro Catholics (2017), Vietnamese Catholics (2015), and Korean Catholics (2015) in the United States.

The Chinese people make up the largest ethnic group in the world (1.3 billion), about 4 million of whom live in the United States. As of 2013, China replaced Mexico as the top country of origin for

---

1   USCCB, *Encountering Christ in Harmony: A Pastoral Response to Our Asian and Pacific Island Brothers and Sisters*, Washington, DC, 2018, p. 5.
2   *Encountering Christ in Harmony*, p. 5.

immigrants to the United States with about 150,000 Chinese immigrating annually.[3] And even though Catholics make up less than 1 percent of the population of China, about 8 percent of Chinese immigrants are Catholic.[4] As such, the Chinese are one of the fastest growing ethnic groups among Catholics in the United States, as seen in **Table 1**. As of 2013, there are an estimated 350,000 ethnic Chinese Catholics in the United States.[5]

This small book is comprised of three sections. The first section describes the history of Chinese Catholics in the United States, when they immigrated, and how their origins and motivations shaped the founding of the many Chinese Catholic communities mostly on the Pacific and Atlantic coasts of the country.

The second section describes the current state of the Chinese Catholic community in the United States, from its structure and clergy to its many lay associations. It goes on to provide cultural insights for ministering to the Chinese American Catholic community, with cultural and linguistic insights, including a suggested calendar of both civic and ecclesial feast days.

The third section touches on the challenges and opportunities that face the Chinese American Catholic community in the twenty-first century, including evangelizing and ministering to the present and future waves of Chinese immigrants and taking the Gospel once again to China, fulfilling our mission to "go into the whole world and proclaim the gospel to every creature" (Mk 16:15).

---

[3] Jensen, Eric. "China Passes Mexico as Top Sending Country of Immigrants to the US." May 1, 2015.
[4] Park, Jerry Z., et al. "Asian Pacific Islander Catholics in the United States: A Preliminary Report." Jan. 2015, p. 32.
[5] Mark Gray, Mary Gautier, and Thomas Gaunt, SJ., *Cultural Diversity in the Church*, June 2014, 10. Washington, DC: Center for the Applied Research in the Apostolate (CARA), 2014.

1. History of Chinese American Catholics

Church leaders may incorrectly assume that all Catholics immigrating to the United States from present-day China, with its tight religious controls and limited contact with the universal Church, need to be more fully formed and assimilated into the more mature Church in the United States. But Christianity in China has a deep and rich history dating back at least a millennium before the Declaration of Independence, to the seventh century, when Syrian Nestorian Christians built the first church in 638 in Chang'an (modern Xian). Western Christianity again made its appearance in China during the thirteenth century, two centuries before Columbus' voyage, when Franciscan missionaries, like Friar Giovanni da Montecorvino, made converts and built churches in what is now Beijing, Quanzhou, Hangzhou, and Yangzhou.

By the time Chinese immigrants began arriving in California during the gold rush of the mid-nineteenth century, Catholicism already had a continuous three-hundred-year history dating back to missionaries like Jesuit Matteo Ricci,[6] "the apostle of China," in the sixteenth century. The first native Chinese priest (and later bishop of Nanjing), Luo Wenzao, had been ordained two hundred years earlier. Lay-led Chinese Catholic communities had learned to be largely self-sufficient for over a century between the expulsion of foreign missionaries in 1721 and the 1840s treaties ending the Opium Wars that reopened China to Western commerce and missionary activity.

Before the 1882 Chinese Exclusion Act was repealed in 1943, opening up the second wave of Chinese immigration to the United States, the first Catholic university, Fu Jen Catholic University, had been established in Beijing in 1924. The first Chinese cardinal, Thomas Tian Gengxin, SVD, (田耕莘), archbishop of Beijing, would

---

6   See section 2.3.1 for more on Matteo Ricci.

soon be named in 1946. And most significantly, tens of thousands of Chinese Catholics had been martyred for their faith during the many episodes of persecutions over the centuries.[7] One remarkable example of these faith-filled martyrs was fourteen-year-old Anna Wang who was beheaded during the anti-foreign, anti-Christian Boxer Rebellion of 1900 for refusing to apostatize. Her final words, while standing up to her torturers, were, "the doors of heaven are open to everyone," followed by the name of Jesus three times.

Even now, as the Chinese continue to come to the United States in a third wave of immigration, which started in the late 1990s with many Catholics among them, the scars of persecution and the blood of martyrs continue to mark their lived experience. Christians in modern China are heavily regulated by the government in how they can worship, how they can organize, how they can pass the faith on to their children, and how they can interact with the universal Catholic Church. Despite these challenges, their perseverance in faith despite persecution and regulation testifies to their deep and tenacious faith in Jesus Christ and his one, holy, catholic, and apostolic Church.

All this is simply to say that the Christian heritage among the Chinese Catholics in the United States, not only goes back a long way and has been a consistent feature during every wave of migration, but this heritage ought to be recognized for the cultural and religious treasure of deep faith that it is and for what it can offer to the broader Catholic Church in the United States.

1.1 CANTONESE-SPEAKING CHINESE CATHOLICS

The Cantonese-speaking Chinese were the first major group of Chinese to come to the United States. Cantonese is the main spoken dialect in the part of southern China that includes the province now known as Guangzhou (formerly referred to as Canton). Cantonese

---

[7] The Church officially recognizes 120 Chinese martyrs who died between the mid-seventeenth century and 1930 with the July 9 feast of St. Augustine Zhao Rong and Companions, who were canonized by Pope John Paul II in 2000. Of the 120 canonized Chinese martyrs, the large majority, 87, were Chinese Catholics (the other 33 being Western missionaries), and were mostly lay people, ranging in age from seven to seventy-nine.

speakers formed the vast majority of the first wave of Chinese migrant workers who fled harsh economic conditions (high taxes leading to loss of land) and political conditions (Taiping Civil War) in the 1840s and 1850s and were drawn to California by the gold rush, some arriving before the famous '49ers. Chinese laborers made up the majority of the workforce on the western branch of the transcontinental railroad, built in the 1860s. When the boom years of the gold rush and the railroad had run their course, many of the Chinese entrepreneur-laborers settled into segregated Chinese ghettos or "Chinatowns" primarily in San Francisco and Sacramento. At the end of the 1850s, one in five residents in San Francisco was Chinese. By 1876, there were about 115,000 Chinese in California.

Ministry to the Chinese community in San Francisco began intermittently with three successive attempts by individual Chinese-speaking priests. The first attempt begun in 1854 was only marginally successful because the native Chinese-speaking priest spoke Mandarin and not the necessary Cantonese. After a short-lived second attempt in 1868, right before the great earthquake, a third attempt lasted eight years between 1881 and 1889 but quickly dissolved when the priest was reassigned as a Vicar Apostolic in China. Only in 1902 was a sustainable Chinese mission established by a group of Paulist Fathers at Old St. Mary's (the former Cathedral) situated in the heart of Chinatown. With the assistance of sisters, many of whom were native Cantonese-speakers, including the Helpers of the Holy Souls from Shanghai, the mission grew to include an elementary school and mission center, ultimately being incorporated into Holy Family Parish in 1927. One of the most successful efforts in San Francisco was the Chinese Language School, established and directed by a respected Chinese herbalist, who was also a recent lay convert. Attracting families, both Catholic and non-Catholic, who wanted their children to retain Chinese language and culture, the school was a powerful instrument to bring Chinese people into the faith.

Another Chinese Catholic mission was started on Mosco Street in New York City in 1909, although it closed in 1920 because of the

Tong wars, which were violent conflicts between Chinese factions. The Chinese community in New York converged on the Church of the Transfiguration in the 1920s while it was being served by the Salesians. The Maryknoll Fathers served this congregation from the 1940s until 2018.

St. Genevieve in Fresno, CA, became the first Chinese national parish in the United States in 1941, having been started in 1934 by Fr. James G. Dowling and the Sisters of the Holy Family as a nursery school for Chinese children in Fresno's Chinatown. St. Bridget in Los Angeles had a similar story, begun by Columban Fr. John Cowhig in 1938 with the encouragement of Chinese Cardinal Paul Yu Pin (于斌), as a nursery school and social center near Chinatown. A similar pattern led to the establishment of St. Therese in Chicago (1940) and Holy Redeemer in Philadelphia (1941).

Since Cantonese-speaking clergy weren't always available, laypersons were a critical part of ministry to the Chinese. In addition to being catechists, they would serve as companion-interpreters with priests on home and hospital visits, at baptisms, weddings, and funerals, and even for the preaching of sermons at Sunday Mass. Lay ministry had been a characteristic feature of the Catholic Church in China, particularly when foreign missionaries were formally expelled from China between 1721 and the 1840s. This tradition has continued among Chinese communities in the United States since the beginning.

Many Cantonese speakers also came during the second wave of migration (1940s-1990s). In 1965, separate quotas were established for Hong Kong, Taiwan, and mainland China. Many well-educated Cantonese-speaking Chinese from Hong Kong came to the United States at this time. A larger proportion of these Hong Kong immigrants were already Catholic, having been educated in Catholic elementary and high schools established by US and European religious orders, such as the Christian Brothers, Jesuits, and Maryknollers. With classroom instruction generally using English but home and daily life using Cantonese, Cantonese American Catholic communities sometimes speak a hybrid "Chinglish" where the basic structure and grammar are Cantonese but any technical or advanced words are in English.

By this time, it was easier for Chinese to assimilate into broader US society. The overt racism they had faced in the late nineteenth century was diminishing. The Chinese Exclusion Act of 1882, the only time any ethnic group has been singled out for discrimination in federal immigration and naturalization law, had been repealed in 1943. The case of a US-born Chinese had gone all the way to the Supreme Court in 1898, enshrining birthright citizenship in the United States. With increased acceptance of the Chinese by this time, their better socio-economic standing compared to the earlier wave, and their greater knowledge of English, this second wave was able to settle beyond the confines of urban Chinatowns.

In San Francisco, Cantonese-language Masses spread to Chinatown's neighboring parishes in the 1970s and to the Richmond and Sunset districts in the 1980s. By 2000, the growth of the Chinese population necessitated Chinese Masses in seven San Francisco area parishes.

The latest wave of Chinese immigration since the late 1990s has had comparatively fewer Cantonese-speakers. As such, Mandarin is becoming the dominant spoken language in Chinese American Catholic communities.

1.2 MANDARIN-SPEAKING CHINESE CATHOLICS

Mandarin, which is based on the northern dialect of the capital city, Beijing, has been the official language of China since the early twentieth century. There are over twenty ways to refer to Mandarin. Among Chinese Americans, the most commonly encountered are *putonghua* (literally, "common speak") for those from mainland China, *guoyu* (literally, "national language") for those from Taiwan and Hong Kong, and "Modern Standard Chinese," the term used by most language-course descriptions in US colleges.

While Mandarin speakers have always been a part of Chinese

immigration to the United States, they were largely outnumbered by Cantonese speakers in the first wave of immigration in the nineteenth through the early twentieth century. Proportionally more Mandarin speakers began immigrating after 1965 when Taiwan received its own immigration quota distinct from China and Hong Kong. At first, Mandarin speakers from Taiwan had the greatest impact on Chinese American communities. Catholicism had spread more broadly in Taiwan, where there was greater international influence and Catholic educational institutions run by foreign missionaries. Like their Hong Kong counterparts, many Taiwanese immigrants were well-educated and socio-economically well off.

The third and latest wave of Chinese immigration starting in the late 1990s has consisted primarily of Mandarin speakers, mostly from mainland China. Economic reforms that have restored China as a major player in the global marketplace have created an increasing wealth disparity among the Chinese population, which is evident in the makeup of this wave's immigrants. There are the economically and geographically mobile, who are establishing primary or secondary homes in the United States on the one hand, the economically or politically marginalized, fleeing desperate circumstances and entering (and remaining in) the United States as undocumented immigrants on the other hand, and everything in between.

Wherever the Chinese have settled in significant numbers, Chinese Catholic communities were founded, including at St. James the Greater Church in Boston (1967); Our Lady of China Pastoral Mission at St. Mary Mother of God in Washington, DC (1982); Ascension Chinese Mission in Houston (1988); Atlanta Chinese Catholic Association (now known as Holy Name of Jesus Chinese Catholic Mission) (1990); and Sacred Heart of Jesus Parish in Dallas (1993). While Chinese Catholic communities established before 1965 predominantly used Cantonese, those established between 1965 and the late 1990s have used a mixture of Cantonese and Mandarin. Since the late 1990s, Chinese parishes nationwide have increased Mandarin-language services, adapting to both the influx of Mandarin-speaking parishioners as well as a greater availability of Mandarin-speaking clergy. In fact, in some communities, Mandarin has become so dominant that Cantonese speakers are finding it difficult to find Cantonese-speaking priests for the Sacrament of Reconciliation.

1.3 FUJIANESE-SPEAKING CHINESE CATHOLICS

The third most significant dialect among Chinese American Catholics is Fujianese, also known as Hokkien. Fujian Province is the coastal southeastern Chinese province opposite Taiwan. Its location on the southern coast and the fact that its capital, Fuzhou, was one of the nineteenth century treaty ports meant that the Fujianese have had comparatively greater contact with Western influence as well as greater opportunities for migration. Hokkien is only one of several dialects spoken in Fujian Province, but has, due to historic migration patterns, become the lingua franca of the Chinese diaspora throughout Southeast Asia, including Singapore, Malaysia, Indonesia, and the Philippines. It is also spoken by many Taiwanese.

Catholicism in Fujian Province traces its origins back to the thirteenth century Franciscans who built churches in Quanzhou. The Dominicans also had a strong influence on Catholic practice in Fujian Province, dating back to their missionary work in the seventeenth century. Many Chinese communities in Fujian Province chose to practice their faith privately when they could not in good conscience follow state regulations of religion beginning in the 1940s and 1950s. Faith communities gathered in private homes, praying together, often without the leadership of ordained clergy. As a result, they were relatively insulated from the liturgical reforms of Vatican II in the 1960s and have cultivated a unique lay-led devotional faith tradition.

While Fujianese speakers have been present among all the waves of Chinese immigrants, their numbers have become increasingly significant in the third wave beginning at the turn of the century. While younger immigrants from Fujian would have learned Mandarin in school, older immigrants would have been schooled in the Fujianese vernacular.

2. Chinese Catholic Community in Contemporary United States

Having traced the history of Catholic Christianity in China as well as Chinese immigration to the United States during the past two centuries, we turn now to the present state of the Chinese American Catholic community. After describing the diversity of structure of Chinese Catholic communities throughout the United States and highlighting various national Chinese American Catholic organizations, practical considerations for ministering to today's Chinese American Catholic communities is provided, including some of the most commonly encountered pastoral concerns facing Chinese American Catholics.

2.1 CHINESE CATHOLIC COMMUNITIES IN THE UNITED STATES TODAY

Today in the United States, Chinese Catholic communities are structured in a variety of ways. Many communities up and down the East and West Coasts are sub-communities within larger territorial parishes such as at Old St. Mary's Cathedral in San Francisco, and Church of the Transfiguration in New York City. Others are structured as national parishes, such as St. Bridget in Los Angeles. But most are stand-alone missions with their own churches or chapels, including Holy Redeemer in Philadelphia, Ascension in Houston, Sacred Heart in Dallas, and most recently, Holy Name in Atlanta. A list of the Chinese Catholic communities in the United States is provided in **Table 2** and a map to visualize the location of these communities is provided in **Figure 1**.

While a handful of communities are fortunate to have Chinese-speaking diocesan priests who reside in their areas, many more rely on the service of itinerant priests, religious priests, retired priests in residence, and/or student priests. In some areas of the country with significant Chinese Catholic populations, Mass in Chinese is not available at all. Not all priests speak all the major varieties of Chinese in common use among the Chinese faithful: Mandarin, Cantonese, and Fujianese.[8] As a result, the elderly faithful who often speak only a single variety of Chinese, particularly either Cantonese or Fujianese, and little or no English, often have a hard time finding priests to hear their confessions.

Since 1979, when Francis Chao (趙振大) of Boston was ordained the first permanent deacon of Chinese descent in the United States, Chinese-speaking permanent deacons have served the American Chinese Catholic communities. Although not too many Chinese-speaking priests are on hand to serve the Sunday communities, almost every location now has a permanent deacon. Houston even has three permanent deacons, as of 2017.

2.2 CHINESE CATHOLIC ASSOCIATIONS IN THE UNITED STATES

Chinese clergy and communities have found it helpful to form a national organization for mutual support and to address issues of common concern. The North American Chinese Catholic Apostolate (originally known as the North American Chinese Catholic Clergy, Religious and Laity Association), founded in 1979 by Fr. Joseph Chiang (江綏) and two other priests in New York, has held annual pastoral conferences across the United States and Canada. The Apostolate has also organized and attended the Worldwide Overseas Chinese Pastoral and Evangelization Conventions. It was recognized by the US Catholic bishops' Conference in 1984 and has received support from Fr. Paul Pang, OFM (彭保祿), the director of the Office for the Promotion of the Overseas Chinese Apostolate of the Vatican's Sacred Congregation for the Evangelization of Peoples (1981-2011).

The US Catholic China Association (*uscatholicchina.org*), formerly

---

8 For more discussion of the varieties of Chinese, see section 2.4.1 Complexities of the Chinese Language.

the US Catholic China Bureau, founded in 1989 by the Society of Jesus and Maryknoll, is another organization composed of clergy, religious, scholars, and lay leaders, dedicated to providing resources and information about the Catholic Church in China. The association offers quarterly bulletins, biennial conferences, and study tours to China, all to promote engagement, cooperation, and service between US Catholics and Chinese Catholics.

Since 1998, The California Chinese Catholic Living Camp (cac-clc.org) has provided Chinese American young adults a weekend of spiritual renewal and fellowship that combines aspects of a retreat with lively and interactive events that foster spiritual growth and practice in living a Christian life.

There are also a variety of national Catholic organizations in the United States with a Chinese language track. For example, Chinese-speaking Cursillo communities can be found in the (arch)dioceses of Galveston-Houston, Los Angeles, Oakland, and New York. Also, the Chinese American Marriage Encounter Association (camea.org) has been serving Chinese American communities since 1989.

2.3 CHINESE CATHOLIC CUSTOMS AND PRACTICES

2.3.1 Inculturation of the Gospel with Confucian Values; Matteo Ricci

Traditional Chinese culture has been built on the foundation of Confucian values for longer than Christianity has been a religion. Confucian philosophy holds the possibility of attaining human perfection in union with heaven (天, tiān) by practicing the virtue of goodness (仁, rén). This innate capacity of human self-transcendence is also present in Taoism and Buddhism and can be summed up in the phrase, lì dì chéng fó (立地成佛), which means give up evil and one can achieve salvation immediately. That goodness is an innate human quality in Confucian thought presents both potential roadblocks and pathways to evangelization. On the one hand, in Confucian thought no divine grace or personal savior is necessary to attain human fulfillment, contrary to Christian doctrine. But on the other hand, innate human goodness and the importance of ethical living dovetail nicely with the Christian doctrine of creation, Catholic social teaching, and the Christian moral life, which would later pave the way for inculturation of the Gospel, when it would arrive in China "in the fullness of time" (cf. Gal 4:4).

Another important component of the Confucian value system is the virtue of filial piety (孝, *xiào*). It emphasizes children's affection and duty toward their parents, elders, and ancestors, whether alive and deceased. Children are expected to be good, respectful, and courteous to their parents, protect their good name, care for them in old age, mourn them in death, and carry out sacrifices for them after death. Filial piety to living ancestors shares much in common with the fourth commandment to honor father and mother. The Confucian impulse to offer sacrifice for ancestors after death is similar to the Catholic impulse to pray for and offer Mass for the deceased, but the particular customs involved in traditional Confucian practice differ because of a different originating worldview. It was these traditional customs of venerating the dead that was the locus of the Chinese Rites Controversy.

Even though the controversy was officially ended when in 1939 Pope Pius XII restored the possibility of integrating ancestral rites in Catholic liturgy, there still isn't a complete acceptance of traditional Chinese ancestral rites, as evidenced by lingering concerns voiced at the 1998 Synod of Asian Bishops. Still, many Chinese Catholic communities in the United States have incorporated ancestral veneration into their celebrations of Chinese New Year, following the recent practice in Taiwan.

Among the many missionaries who adapted to China's language, dress, culture, and traditions were St. Joseph Freinademetz, who wrote a catechism in Chinese and was the first missionary to China to be canonized, and Fr. Vincent Lebbe, a Lazarist (Vincentian) priest whose advocacy was instrumental in the consecration and appointment of native Chinese bishops in the 1920s. But there was perhaps no missionary to China who better understood the importance of respecting China's ancient culture and traditions more than Servant of God Matteo Ricci, the famed Jesuit "apostle of China."

Ricci's first step upon arriving in China was an intense multi-year study of Chinese language and culture. With this knowledge he was able to explain the Gospel using familiar Chinese ideas and terminology, presenting Christianity not as new and foreign, but as the perfection of existing Chinese belief in God and heaven. This is very similar to St. Paul's use of the "Unknown God" when proclaiming the Gospel to the people of Athens (Acts 17:23). With deep respect for the heritage of Confucian wisdom, Ricci Christianized those elements of traditional Confucian practice that were compatible with the faith but rejected those that were not. The Jesuits even advocated for and received permission to celebrate the liturgy in Chinese in 1615, when the use of the vernacular was strictly prohibited in Europe in the aftermath of the Protestant Reformation. Ricci and his collaborators were so successful that he is one of the few foreigners buried in Imperial Beijing. To this day, the name of Matteo Ricci (利瑪竇, "Li Madou") is one of few Western figures well known among the Chinese, both Christian and non-Christian alike.

Ricci has been hailed as an exemplar of inculturation by the three most recent popes. St. John Paul II extolled Ricci's missionary work in China pointing to the "deep empathy he cultivated towards the whole history, culture and tradition of the Chinese people."[9] Ricci's inculturation of the Gospel into the deeply rooted Chinese culture followed in the footsteps of the Fathers of early Church when they brought the Gospel of Jesus Christ to Greco-Roman culture. Pope Benedict XVI called Ricci "a true protagonist of Gospel proclamation in China in the modern age" and "a unique case of a felicitous synthesis between the proclamation of the Gospel and the dialogue with the

---

9 Pope John Paul II, Message to the International Conference Commemorating the Fourth Centenary of the Arrival in Beijing of Fr. Matteo Ricci, Oct. 2001.

culture of the people to whom he brought it."[10] Pope Francis likewise has repeatedly held up Ricci, a fellow Jesuit, as an exemplary evangelist during media interviews and unscripted conversations. Fr. Matteo Ricci is indeed a model of successful inculturation of the Gospel. His legacy provides both a model for Christian evangelization among Chinese Americans and a positive point of contact between Chinese and Western culture.

2.3.2 Marian Devotion

Marian devotion plays an important part in the faith lives of Chinese Catholics. Devotions like the Rosary were an integral part of prayer during the many episodes when Chinese Catholic communities did not have access to clergy and were led by lay catechists and elders.

In addition to celebrating universal Marian feast days, for example, New York's Transfiguration Church's procession for the Feast of the Assumption of the Blessed Virgin Mary, the Chinese have their own unique Marian feasts. Of particular noteworthiness are the devotions to Mary under the titles of Our Lady of Sheshan and Our Lady of Donglu. Our Lady of Sheshan is a basilica in the suburbs of Shanghai. Originally a retreat center and chapel dedicated to Our Lady Help of Christians, a basilica was completed at the site in 1873 in thanksgiving for Our Lady's protection of Shanghai from the ravages of the Taiping Civil War (1850-1864). In 1874, Pope Pius IX granted a plenary indulgence to pilgrims who visit the shrine during the month of May. It has since become a pilgrimage site for Chinese Catholics from all over China and Southeast Asia, particularly on May 1 and May 24, the feast of Our Lady Help of Christians. In 2007, Pope Benedict XVI established May 24, the feast of Our Lady Help of Christians, as a World Day of Prayer for the Church in China.

Our Lady of Donglu is another pilgrimage site for Chinese Catholics. When the small village of Donglu in Hebei Province, with

---

10   Pope Benedict XVI, Address on the Occasion of the 400th Anniversary of the Death of Fr. Matteo Ricci, May 2010.

about a thousand Catholics, was attacked by ten thousand soldiers during the Boxer Rebellion in 1900, an apparition of Our Lady reportedly chased them away, saving the village. Annual processions of up to a hundred thousand people were held in Donglu until the gathering was suppressed by government authorities in 1997. The feast day was chosen by the Chinese bishops and is celebrated on the vigil of the second Sunday of May (Mother's Day). Later apparitions of Mary have been reported at the Donglu shrine as recently as 1995. When a church was built at the site, an image was commissioned representing Mary in the robes of a Chinese empress and carrying the Christ child, which has come to be known as Our Lady of China.

A mosaic in honor of Our Lady of China was dedicated at the Basilica of the National Shrine of the Immaculate Conception in Washington, DC, in 2002. Rather than a replica of the original image of Our Lady of China from Donglu, a more contemporary image commissioned by Cardinal Tian in the 1950s was selected.

2.3.3 Special Days on the Chinese Calendar

Just as US parishes often plan special liturgies and parish events for US civic holidays like the Fourth of July or Thanksgiving that are not found on the Roman liturgical calendar, it would be fitting to acknowledge and celebrate many of the key Chinese festivals, especially Chinese New Year, when planning liturgies for a Chinese American community. The traditional Chinese calendar is a lunisolar calendar, with the reckoning of dates for major festivals following the movements of both the sun and the moon. Chinese festivals, therefore, typically fall on different days of the Gregorian calendar each year. **Table 3** lists the most important Chinese festivals and their approximate dates on the Gregorian calendar along with a brief description of the traditional activities and foods that accompany each festival.

Similarly, as US parishes would recognize and celebrate the memorials of US saints such as St. Elizabeth Ann Seton, St. Katharine Drexel, St. Damien of Molokai, and St. Kateri Tekakwitha, it is also fitting to celebrate the memorials of some of the most important and widely venerated Chinese saints. These are listed in **Table 4** with their feast days on the Gregorian calendar and a brief description.

2.3.4 Colors and Numbers in Chinese Culture

Awareness of the cultural interpretation of colors and numbers is another important aspect of ministering to traditional Chinese communities in liturgical contexts. Red is the color of celebration and good fortune, featuring prominently in decorations and clothing connected to festivities such as the Chinese New Year and traditional Chinese weddings. Many traditional Chinese will therefore be particularly drawn in when red is used as the liturgical color, like on feasts of the martyrs or on Pentecost. On Palm Sunday and Good Friday when red is used at these two liturgies commemorating Christ's Passion and Death, traditional Chinese sensibility would find it incongruent and perhaps even improper to use the color of happiness and good fortune when focusing on suffering and death. Pastors could use this occasion as an opportunity for catechesis about Catholic liturgical colors.

White is the color of death and mourning, as it is reminiscent of the pallid hue that overcomes the body after death. This can be quite confusing on a subconscious visceral level, even to the well-catechized, especially at funerals or throughout the Easter season when white is intended to symbolize life and resurrection but could be construed to mean death and mourning.

Green is associated with health and prosperity, which is very similar to the Roman Catholic liturgical meaning of life in Christ. Wearing a green hat, however, has the idiomatic meaning that one's spouse is unfaithful. This may be pertinent to a bishop's choice of mitre during Ordinary Time. Violet tends not to cause problems as its traditional Chinese meanings of divinity and immortality are different but not antithetical to its liturgical use in Advent, Lent, and the Sacrament of Reconciliation.

Just as certain numbers have special significance biblically and culturally in the West—for example, three and seven being good numbers; six and thirteen being a little nefarious—so too numbers have important meaning among the Chinese, especially the Cantonese. Three, six, eight, thirteen, and eighteen are particularly good numbers representing good fortune, growth, and prosperity. Four, seven, fourteen, and twenty-four are inauspicious numbers representing death. The biblical and cultural significance of numbers can be considerations not only in homiletics but also for selecting event dates in a way that will maximize participation.

2.4 PASTORAL CONSIDERATIONS FOR MINISTERING TO CHINESE AMERICANS

2.4.1 Complexities of the Chinese Language

Chinese is considered a single language because there is only one written form, which is written Mandarin. Cantonese, Fujianese, and all other dialects have no written form of their own. Instead, the other dialects must essentially be written in Mandarin. When Cantonese persons, for example, read from a text, they have two options. They can pronounce the text character-by-character with Cantonese cognates, resulting in a stilted-sounding spoken Cantonese that is strictly faithful to the written text. This method assures fidelity to the approved liturgical translation when proclaiming Sacred Scripture during liturgy. Alternatively, they can translate on-the-go to more colloquial Cantonese usage at the risk of potentially deviating from the written text. This is more suitable for situations like prayer meetings, catechesis, and homilies.

While there is only one written Chinese language, since the 1950s there have been two forms of written Chinese: traditional characters and simplified characters. In an attempt to modernize and increase efficiency of the character-based language, Mao's regime introduced simplified characters in the 1950s. Several further rounds of revisions since then have resulted in Modern Standard Chinese that uses simplified characters. It is not that the text has been simplified like might be done when creating a children's Bible, for example. Rather each pictogram, representing a Chinese word, was simplified in the sense that it had a reduction in the number of strokes it takes to write it.

Chinese-language written resources, like Bibles and catechetical texts, can be found in both traditional and simplified characters. Cantonese-speakers and Taiwanese Mandarin-speakers typically read traditional characters. Mandarin-speakers from mainland China will generally read simplified characters. If searching for Catholic Bibles online, the currently approved Catholic version for liturgical use is the Studium Biblicum translation done by Bl. Gabriele Allegra, OFM, and his team between 1945 and 1968. Also available is a pastoral translation into modern Chinese, completed in 1998 by the Claretians under the direction of Fr. Bernard Hurault. On the internet, the most commonly spotted translation is the Chinese Union Version, which is the most widely used Protestant translation, recently updated in 2010.

Many Sunday communities purchase missalettes and hymnals from China, Hong Kong, and mainland China. For example, the Catholic Centre in Hong Kong (*http://www.catholiccentre.org.hk*), a ministry of the Catholic Diocese of Hong Kong, provides access to Chinese language materials, with customer service in both Chinese and English. Increasingly the laity as well as clergy utilize free electronic books and phone apps, including the *Catechism of the Catholic Church* and iBreviarium, which offers morning and evening prayers, Mass readings, saints of the day, and the entire Bible in both traditional and simplified characters. Thanks to the San Jose Chinese Catholic Mission, a Chinese-English parallel Bible for Catholics was published by the Archdiocese of San Francisco (2013-New Testament; 2016-Old Testament) as a tool for evangelization as well as for use among Catholics.

As of this writing, no Catholic radio or television network in the United States provides daily programs in Chinese. Vatican Radio (*radiovaticana.va*) has Chinese language media resources.

One can also find private broadcast media groups in Canada with Chinese content for Catholics.

2.4.2 Generational Differences and Pastoral Needs

The Chinese American Catholic community is not a monolithic group with a homogeneous set of pastoral needs. In addition to differences between place of family origin (e.g., Taiwan, Hong Kong, Macao, or mainland China), the variety of Chinese spoken (primarily Mandarin, Cantonese, or Fujianese), and socioeconomic circumstances, it is important to note the differences in pastoral needs between foreign-born and native-born Chinese Americans. First generation, foreign-born Catholic immigrants tend to see the Chinese parish as a cultural and spiritual connection to their home countries. The familiarity of worship in their native tongue and being surrounded with those who are linguistically and culturally similar make the Chinese parish a source of stability and comfort for their lives that otherwise feel uprooted and anxious. They tend to see their participation in the Chinese parish as an important way of preserving their heritage and passing it on to their children.

The second-generation, native-born children of the first, tend to have a very different experience. Once they reach school age, English tends to become their primary language, no matter what combination of English, Chinese, or Chinglish is spoken in the home. As such, their interior thoughts, including their prayers, are typically in English. The native-born tend to gravitate toward English-speaking liturgies and parish activities, even if they are fluent in Chinese. They don't experience complete acceptance in US culture, nor do they feel that they truly belong among the first-generation immigrants, even of the same age, who cling to an overseas way of life. They struggle to please their parents, who often insist that they successfully assimilate into US culture while still retaining their Chinese heritage, language, and customs—seemingly contradictory goals. Any resentment this causes may be transferred to their experience of the faith and how they succeed or fail to internalize it. Caught inexorably between two cultures, they find solace and understanding among those in their same second-generation situation.

Even more caught-in-the-middle are the so called 1.5-generation immigrants, those who immigrated around their early-teenage years. They tend to become the most bilingual and bicultural and can be key persons in bridging the gap between the immigrant generations. On the downside, their biculturality can result in their sometimes being the least settled, feeling internally ambivalent about identity and culture.

Given these immigrant generation dynamics, similar to those in many immigrant communities, it is not uncommon to find ministries in Chinese American parishes duplicated along language lines. A Chinese-speaking youth group, formed by those seeking to preserve Chinese identity, can often be found at the same parish alongside an English-speaking Chinese youth group, composed of those oriented toward assimilation. Similar dynamics can be operative for young adult groups, RCIA, small groups, and adult faith formation. While individuals seek a place of belonging within smaller parish subgroups, the differences of language, socioeconomics, and immigrant generation are ultimately not significant barriers to parish unity. The Chinese community naturally comes together around parish-wide events including liturgy and cultural festivals,[11] especially when food is shared.

---

11   For more information on Chinese festivals, see Table 3: Calendar of Key Chinese Festivals.

3. Chinese American Catholic Community: Opportunities and Future Directions

The first two sections have looked at the Chinese American Catholic community, past and present. In this last and briefest of the three primary sections of this small book, we look to the future of the Chinese American Catholic community, both in terms of the future of evangelization of and ministry to the Chinese American community and also in terms of how the Church can assist the work of evangelizing China itself.

3.1 MINISTERING TO CHINESE IMMIGRANTS

"You shall treat the alien who resides with you no differently than the natives born among you; you shall love the alien as yourself; for you too were once aliens in the land of Egypt." (Lv 19:34)

While some Chinese immigrants have been attracted to and have converted to Christianity, many more have yet to hear and accept the Gospel. Just as our brother bishops in Asia promoted a triple dialogue—"with the poor, with cultures, and with religions"[12]—we recommend the proclamation of Jesus Christ to the millions of Chinese Americans, Catholics and non-Catholics, in a dialogical manner amidst a diversity of beliefs, cultures, and socio-political structures. We must speak with and learn from millions of victims of injustice, as well as the spiritualities and cultures that have nurtured the Chinese for ages. Only then will the Church be perceived as an accompanying presence to the Chinese American community.

---

12 Kroeger, James H. "Dialogue: Interpretive Key for the Life of the Church in Asia." FABC Papers no. 130. May 2010. http://www.fabc.org/fabc%20papers/FABC%20paper%20130.pdf. Accessed Apr. 27, 2018. p. 2

3.1.1 Welcoming the Immigrant

While the focus of the media and public policy surrounding undocumented immigrants largely centers on Hispanic groups, the Chinese are not exempt from this conversation. In fact, with an estimated 268,000 undocumented Chinese immigrants nationwide as of 2017, mainland China ranks fifth among countries of origin of undocumented immigrants in the United States, the highest of any country outside Mexico and Central America.[13] Chinese American Catholic communities, therefore, are important voices in the constantly evolving national debate on immigration reform, particularly with respect to the so-called "dreamers."

3.1.2 Separated Families, Remarriage, Interracial Marriage

In some instances, Chinese immigrants leave family in their homeland and begin new lives in the United States, sometimes even starting second families with second spouses without first dissolving or annulling previous marriages. This is particularly true of undocumented immigrants. This is obviously a pastoral concern, particularly in the context of RCIA.

Also noteworthy is that Asians have the highest rate of interracial marriage in the United States, hovering at about 30 percent.[14] This presents a unique pastoral need for ministry to interracial and interfaith marriages.

3.1.3 Ministering to Working Immigrants

Like myriad immigrants before them, many Chinese American immigrants must work long hours at strenuous manual jobs, even on weekends. Many are not able to keep their jobs and regularly join a

---

13   Yee, Vivian, et al. "Here's the Reality About Illegal Immigrants in the United States." The New York Times, Mar. 6, 2017, *www.nytimes.com/interactive/2017/03/06/us/politics/undocumented-illegal-immigrants.html*. Accessed Apr. 9, 2018.

14   Livingston, Gretchen, and Anna Brown. "Intermarriage in the U.S. 50 Years after Loving v. Virginia." May 18, 2017, *www.pewsocialtrends.org/2017/05/18/1-trends-and-patterns-in-intermarriage/*. Accessed Apr. 11, 2018.

Christian community for liturgy, prayer, or fellowship on Saturday evening or Sunday, except for major solemnities like Christmas and Easter. Ministering to this group will require creative approaches on weekdays and can take advantage of technology. For example, Old St. Patrick in New York City keeps its doors open during weekdays and offers a weekday bible study by phone and through internet streaming apps. Although not a liturgical feast day, Thanksgiving Day, especially in the morning, is sometimes the one day of the year that all immigrant wage earners are able to have a break from work. This can be an ideal day for a morning liturgy and community activities targeted to the immigrant community.

3.2 VOCATIONS, EVANGELIZATION, AND MINISTRY

"The harvest is abundant but the laborers are few; so ask the master of the harvest to send out laborers for his harvest."
(Mt 9:37-38)

"You will be my witnesses . . . to the ends of the earth." (Acts 1:8)

3.2.1 Vocations

Due to the one-child policy, Chinese men outnumber women both in China and consequently also in the United States.[15] Even with Chinese men often unable to find wives, Chinese Catholic parents may be reluctant to offer up their only sons for service in the Church since the sons carry the family name in the Chinese tradition. Compared to the Vietnamese, the number of Chinese priests in the United States is much smaller. However, in Texas alone there are four relatively young priests of Chinese descent. Pastors may want to nurture young men and women of Chinese descent to discern vocations to the priesthood and consecrated life. Priests and parents may also encourage US-born Chinese to learn the language and

---

15   Koetse, Manya. "China now has 33.5 million more men than women." Jan. 23, 2017, *www.whatsonweibo.com/china-now-335-million-men-women/*. Accessed Apr. 27, 2018.

tradition. If more US residents learn and speak Chinese, they may be able to effectively evangelize and minister instead of relying only on foreign-born clergy.

Speaking of consecrated life, some men and women of Chinese descent are found in religious communities, including the Dominicans and Franciscans. Some have served leadership roles in southern California and New Jersey. Talented religious such as Sr. Joanna Chan, MM, (陳尹瑩) have contributed in multiple ways to the Church in the United States.

3.2.2 Indirect Missionary Work in China

Direct missionary work in China by foreigners is not permitted by the Chinese government. However, some US residents have found indirect ways to share their faith in China. For example, US seminarians studying at the North American College in Rome, representing several US dioceses, spent a summer teaching English at Jilin Medical University in Jilin City with English professor Brian Barrons, who also happens to be a Maryknoll priest.[16] While they could not directly proselytize, they were able to share their own life stories and experiences in response to the inevitable student questions and were thereby able to share the story of Jesus with their students. These types of indirect missionary efforts can be quite successful when efforts are made to connect inquirers with their local parishes.

3.2.3 Evangelizing Chinese Students

There is another way to indirectly evangelize China. Over the past decade or so, the rising mobility of the middle class in China has led Chinese parents to increasingly seek educational opportunities for their children abroad, including in the United States. While many Chinese have been coming to the United States for post-secondary education since the 1960s, nowadays, they are increasingly coming

---

16   Mariscal, Jésus. "Evangelizing China." *Roman Echoes* 20(2). 2015. Pages 38-39.

as early as high school freshmen, often unaccompanied, creating a unique pastoral opportunity for Catholic schools across the country to welcome these Chinese students, many of whom have never heard the Gospel and who often plan to return to China following their education. Bishop Walsh School in Cumberland, MD, named for the Maryknoll missionary bishop of Jiangmen, is one such school, which has embraced continuing the mission of its namesake in bringing the Gospel to the Chinese people (*http://bishopwalsh.org/admissions/internationalstudents*). As of 2013, there are about 6,500 Chinese students attending Catholic high schools in the United States.[17] If they embrace Christianity and return to China, they will be uniquely positioned to spread the Gospel in China in a way no foreign missionary has been able to do for the last seventy years.

Evangelization of Chinese youth is not limited to foreign students. Many Chinese immigrants, whether or not they are Catholic, choose to send their children to Catholic schools. They are attracted by the reputation for excellence and discipline that they often first encountered in missionary schools in their countries of origin. While many Catholic schools struggle financially to survive, the Transfiguration School in New York City outgrew itself due to demand from Chinese immigrant families.

The need to focus efforts on the evangelization of Chinese youth is more acute since the recent increase of restrictions on ministry to youth in China. In February 2018, new regulations were enforced in China, including a ban on minors entering churches.[18] While enforcement will likely vary depending on the particular relationship between the local government and the local church, reports have been surfacing that in some jurisdictions, in addition to banning youth attendance in church, no Sunday school may be taught, and no religious education can be offered in summer camps. Pastors and faith formation teams may want to be more aware of the need to

---

17   Zavagnin, Anthony J. "Filling Empty Seats." *America: The Jesuit Review*, 215(14). Oct. 31, 2016.
18   Catholic News Service. "Chinese priests ordered to put up signs banning children from churches." *http://www.catholicherald.co.uk/news/2018/02/09/chinese-priests-ordered-to-put-up-signs-banning-children-from-churches/*. Feb 9, 2018. Accessed Apr. 27, 2018.

help Catholics from mainland China to grow in faith and reason, especially in the areas of how to live out the Christian life in the United States.

3.2.4 Supporting the Church in China

Since the 1920s, Chinese clergy and religious have traveled to the United States for education and training. More recently, since 1991, the Maryknoll Fathers and Brothers have helped train over 138 Chinese church leaders through advanced degree programs in the United States through their program called the China Educators and Formators Project. There were graduates in canon law, Scripture, moral theology, liturgy, spiritual direction, church history, pastoral counseling, family therapy, and social work. Many participants have returned to China to serve as bishops, seminary rectors, professors, and in other positions of pastoral leadership. Continuing efforts in this area are still needed to assist the Church in China. While the program is about offering opportunities for advanced studies, project participants also offer pastoral services to local Chinese Catholic communities in dioceses where they study.

Besides the Maryknoll China Project, the Vincentians have been running the Chinese Leadership Initiative, a four-week leadership development program each summer since 2012 for clergy and religious sisters.

3.3 CHINESE CATHOLICS ENRICH THE CHURCH IN THE UNITED STATES

"There are different kinds of spiritual gifts but the same Spirit."
(1 Cor 12:4)

Chinese American Christians bring distinctive characteristics and values to the Church in the United States that can be celebrated and can enrich the wider Church. In a time when marriage, family, and the culture of life are under attack in the United States, Chinese

American Christians, whose families live together multi-generationally, typically three and often four generations in the same household, bear witness to the centrality of family and the dignity of life in all its stages, especially the elderly.

We are also experiencing a prolonged period in the Church in the United States where the intellectual faith knowledge of the average Catholic has declined compared to earlier generations. Chinese American Catholics, with a strong cultural value for education and knowledge, can bear witness to the need and benefit of deepening intellectual knowledge of the faith.

Many Chinese Catholic immigrants are coming from political circumstances where they have not enjoyed religious freedom as we do in the United States. Discrimination, persecution, repression, and sometimes even martyrdom have been the lived experience of Chinese immigrants from mainland China. Their witness of perseverance in faith and the centrality of life in Christ, despite the risk, brings a perspective on discipleship that is sorely needed in contemporary US culture, which is quickly secularizing.

Conclusion

"As a body is one though it has many parts, and all the parts of the body, though many, are one body, so also Christ."
(1 Cor 12:12)

Chinese Catholics are an integral part of the contemporary Church in the United States and their role in it will only grow as the world becomes increasingly globalized. Chinese Catholics have a rich history of faith, having survived multiple episodes of growth and evangelization as well as persecution and martyrdom. Chinese Catholics have adapted the unchanging Gospel of Jesus Christ to their rich and ancient culture founded on Confucian values, proving that the Good News is for everyone in all times and places.

Chinese Catholics, like many immigrant groups before them, face a number of pastoral challenges as immigrants. But even as Chinese Catholics seek to nurture their faith in the Catholic Church in the United States, they are also active participants in building the Kingdom in their parishes and communities. Their strong family values, history of lay leadership, and experiences of persecution and martyrdom offer an important witness to the broader contemporary Catholic Church in the United States.

Chinese American Catholics are in a unique position to continue the mission of evangelization to the billion-plus Chinese worldwide who have not heard the Good News of Jesus Christ. It is our hope that this small book will serve as one small step toward mutual understanding and greater unity of Chinese Catholics within the Church in the United States. With this greater unity, not only will the Church in the United States be better able to serve the needs of the Chinese faithful, but Chinese American Catholics will better see how they can enrich the Church in the United States as partners in evangelization and share the Good News with all the Chinese worldwide.

Our Lady of China, pray for us.

FIGURE 1. MAP OF CHINESE CATHOLIC COMMUNITIES IN THE UNITED STATES

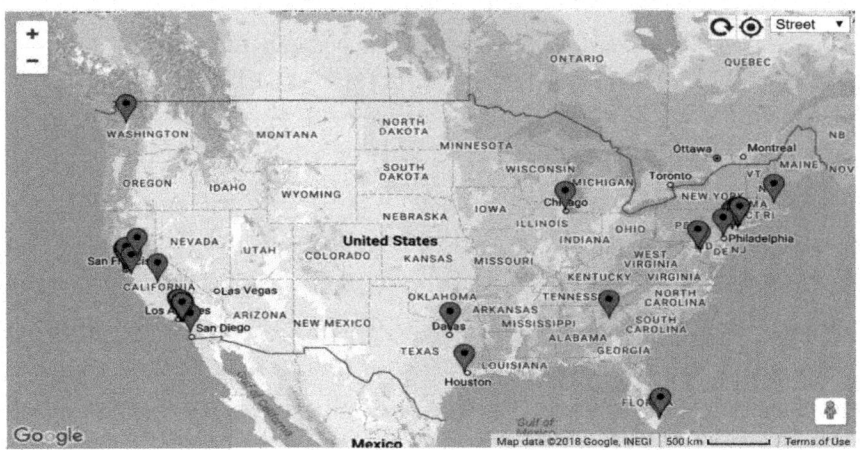

TABLE 1. US CATHOLIC POPULATION, RACE, ETHNICITY, AND BIRTHPLACE ESTIMATES, 2013.[19]

	Population	Catholic Population
White (non-Hispanic)	201,603,212	43,546,293
Black, African American, African, Afro-Caribbean	39,875,893	2,990,692
Black, African American, African, Afro-Caribbean (non-Hispanic)	38,602,187	2,142,422
Born in Africa	1,280,200	337,973
Asian, Native Hawaiian, Pacific Islander *	15,584,203	2,976,583
Filipino	3,499,921	2,267,949
Vietnamese	1,779,679	494,750
Chinese	4,107,621	349,148
Korean	1,748,324	204,554
Native Hawaiian/Pacific Islander	553,144	151,009
Indian	3,260,460	149,981
Japanese	1,336,000	57,448
Hispanic, Latino	51,704,967	30,454,225
Native-born	30,639,814	16,422,941
Foreign-born	21,065,153	14,029,392
American Indian, Alaskan Native	3,003,546	549,649

* Due to significant numbers of Asian American, Native Hawaiian, and Pacific Islander Americans having multiple racial, ethnic, and ancestral identities, totals for sub-groups do not add to the total Asian American, Native Hawaiian, and Pacific Islander group population number.

---

19   Mark Gray, Mary Gautier, and Thomas Gaunt, SJ. *Cultural Diversity in the Church*, June 2014, 10. Washington, DC: Center for the Applied Research in the Apostolate (CARA), 2014.

TABLE 2. CHINESE CATHOLIC COMMUNITIES IN THE UNITED STATES

Note: List of Chinese Catholic communities is arranged by descending zip code.

Our Lady of Mt. Virgin Church	1531 Bradner Pl S	Seattle	WA	98144
Cathedral of the Blessed Sacrament	1017 11th St	Sacramento	CA	95814
San Jose Chinese Catholic Mission—St. Clare's Church	725 Washington St	Santa Clara	CA	95050
St. Paul's Church—Our Mary's House of Mercy	1845 Church Ln	San Pablo	CA	94806
St. Leo Church	176 Ridgeway Ave	Oakland	CA	94611
Our Lady of the Rosary Church	703 C St	Union City	CA	94587
St. Joseph Church	43148 Mission Blvd	Fremont	CA	94539
St. Matthew Church	1 Notre Dame Ave	San Mateo	CA	94402
Ss. Peter & Paul Church	666 Filbert St	San Francisco	CA	94133
Holy Name of Jesus	3240 Lawton St	San Francisco	CA	94122
St. Anne of the Sunset Church	850 Judah St	San Francisco	CA	94122
St. Monica Church	470 24th St	San Francisco	CA	94121
Old St. Mary's Cathedral—Holy Family Chinese Mission	660 California St	San Francisco	CA	94108
St. Genevieve's Church	1127 Tulare St	Fresno	CA	93706
Christ Cathedral—Large Gallery	13280 Chapman Ave	Garden Grove	CA	92840
Sacred Heart Mission	10852 Harcourt Ave	Anaheim	CA	92804
St. Thomas More Chinese Ministry	51 Marketplace	Irvine	CA	92602

St. Therese of Carmel	4355 Del Mar Trails Rd	San Diego	CA	92130
St. Thomas Aquinas Church	1501 S Atlantic Blvd	Monterey Park	CA	91754
St. Elizabeth Ann Seton Church	1835 Larkvane Rd	Rowland Heights	CA	91748
Holy Family	18708 S Clarksdale Ave	Artesia	CA	90701
St. Bridget Chinese Catholic Church	510 Cottage Home St	Los Angeles	CA	90012
Ascension Chinese Mission	4605 Jetty Ln	Houston	TX	77072
Sacred Heart of Jesus Chinese Parish	4201 14th St	Plano	TX	75074
St. Therese Chinese Catholic Mission	218 W Alexander St	Chicago	IL	60616
St. Jerome Church	2533 SW 9th Ave	Ft. Lauderdale	FL	33315
St. Thomas University—Chapel of St. Anthony	16401 NW 37th Ave	Miami Gardens	FL	33054
Holy Name of Jesus Chinese Catholic Mission	5395 Light Circle NW	Norcross	GA	30071
Our Lady of China Pastoral Mission—St. Mary's Church	520 Veirs Mill Rd	Rockville	MD	20852
Our Lady of China Pastoral Mission—St. Mary Mother of God Church	727 Fifth St	Washington	DC	20001
Holy Redeemer Chinese Catholic Church	915 Vine St	Philadelphia	PA	19107
St. Michael's Church	138-65 Barclay Ave	Queens	NY	11355
St. John Vianney Catholic Church	140-10 34th Ave	Flushing	NY	11354
St. Agatha Church	702 48th St	Brooklyn	NY	11220
Basilica of Our Lady of Perpetual Help	526 59th St	Brooklyn	NY	11220

Basilica of Regina Pacis—St. Joseph Chapel	6301 14th Ave	Brooklyn	NY	11219
Church of the Transfiguration	29 Mott St	New York	NY	10013
Basilica of St. Patrick's Old Cathedral	263 Mulberry St	New York	NY	10012
St. Teresa Church	141 Henry St	New York	NY	10002
Chinese Catholic Spiritual Center	PO Box 1514	Highland Park	NJ	08904
Our Lady of Mt. Virgin Church	650 Harris Ave	Middlesex	NJ	08846
New Jersey Chinese Catholic Apostolate—Holy Cross Church	16 Church Square	Harrison	NJ	07029
Chinese Catholic Pastoral Center—St. James the Greater Church	125 Harrison Ave	Boston	MA	02111

Source: North American Chinese Catholic Apostolate.

TABLE 3. CALENDAR OF KEY CHINESE FESTIVALS

Date	Name	Description
Late Jan.–Early Feb.	Chinese New Year (農曆新年) (Spring Festival, 春節) (first day of first month on the Chinese calendar)	The most important traditional festival on the Chinese calendar, this is a fortnight-long event marked by family meals, where the dishes symbolize wishes for the new year, such as fish for prosperity and copious decorations in auspicious red. Each year is marked by one of twelve animals in the zodiac cycle. Traditional activities include firecrackers, dragon dances, giving red envelopes, and ancestral veneration. This festival is shared with the Vietnamese[20] and Koreans.[21]
Mid-Feb.–Early Mar.	Lantern Festival (元宵節) (fifteenth day of first month)	The last day of the Chinese New Year festival takes place on the first full moon of the year. Falling after the week-long New Year's public holiday, most people are not able to celebrate this day with family. Traditional activities include enjoying lanterns, lion dances, and eating ball-shaped dumplings to symbolize togetherness.

---

20   United States Conference of Catholic Bishops, Committee on Cultural Diversity in the Church, Subcommittee on Asian and Pacific Island Affairs. *Resettling in Place: A Vietnamese American Catholic Experience.* Washington, DC: USCCB. 2014.

21   United States Conference of Catholic Bishops, Committee on Cultural Diversity in the Church, Subcommittee on Asian and Pacific Island Affairs. *Harmony in Faith: Korean American Catholics.* Washington, DC: USCCB. 2014.

Apr. 4, 5, or 6	Qingming (Ching Ming) Festival (清明節), Tomb-Sweeping Day (fifteenth day after the Spring Equinox)	A day to remember and honor ancestors by cleaning the graves of ancestors.
Mid-June	Dragon Boat Festival (端午節) (fifth day of fifth month)	Honors a revered poet, Qu Yuan (343-278 BC). Traditional activities include eating sticky rice dumplings and dragon boat races.
Late Aug.-Mid-Sept.	Double Ninth Festival (ninth day of ninth month)	Traditionally, a day to visit the graves of ancestors. More recently, a day to honor and respect elders, living and deceased.
Late Sept.-Early Oct.	Mid-Autumn Festival (中秋節) (fifteenth day of eighth month)	Harvest Festival during the full moon is for gathering friends and family, giving thanks for the harvest, and praying for good fortune. Traditional activities include moon gazing and eating moon cakes. This festival is also shared with the Vietnamese and Koreans.
Dec. 22	Winter Solstice (冬至)	Sometimes called "Chinese Thanksgiving." Traditional activities include family gatherings, honoring ancestors, and eating ball-shaped dumplings.

Some Chinese festivals follow a lunar calendar and thus, like Passover and Easter, their dates vary each year on the Gregorian calendar, the contemporary international standard calendar used in the United States.

TABLE 4. CALENDAR OF CHINESE LITURGICAL FEASTS

This is a partial listing of Chinese saints, blesseds, and servants of God in the Catholic Church. For a comprehensive listing of Asian and Pacific Island (API) Catholic saints and blesseds, including Chinese saints and blesseds, please visit the website of the USCCB's Subcommittee of Asian and Pacific Island Affairs at *https://www.usccb.org/committees/asian-and-pacific-island-affairs*. An updated downloadable PDF of API saints will become available soon under "Resources."

Jan. 26		Blessed Gabriele Allegra, OFM (雷永明)	(1907-1976) Known as the "Chinese St. Jerome," Italian Franciscan friar and biblical scholar, founded the Studium Biblicum Franciscanum in Beijing in 1945 to translate the Scriptures into Chinese. Moved to Kowloon, Hong Kong, in 1948 due to the Chinese civil war. With a group of fellow Franciscans, published the translation from Hebrew, Aramaic, and Greek manuscripts in phases from 1948 to 1968. This translation is now considered by many as "the Chinese Bible" for Catholics. His cause for canonization was begun by Bishop John Wu of Hong Kong in 1984. He was declared venerable in 1994 and beatified in 2012.

Jan. 28	St. Joseph Freinademetz, SVD (聖福若瑟)	(1852-1908) Austrian priest of the Society of the Divine Word, missionary to Shandong Province, China. Wrote a catechism in Chinese. Beatified in 1975. Canonized in 2003.
Vigil of Second Sunday of May (Mother's Day)	Our Lady of China (中華聖母)	Apparition of Our Lady who chased away attacking soldiers from the village of Donglu, Hebei, in 1900 during the Boxer Rebellion. Image of Our Lady, Queen of China was promulgated in 1928. Later apparitions of Mary at the shrine built to honor Mary in Donglu were reported as recently as 1995.

May 11	Servant of God Matteo Ricci, SJ (利瑪竇)	(1552-1610) Italian Jesuit priest often called the "apostle of China." Brought the Gospel to the imperial court of Beijing in 1601 as the first Westerner to enter the Forbidden City. Using expertise in Western science, mathematics, and mapmaking, received patronage of the imperial court, making many converts among the Chinese elite with the help of a handful of companions. Declared Servant of God in 1984. While not yet a blessed or saint, the Chinese faithful are encouraged to pray for his canonization. May 11 is the anniversary of his death.

May 24	Our Lady of Sheshan (佘山聖母), Our Lady Help of Christians	Basilica built in a western suburb of Shanghai to honor Our Lady's protection of Shanghai during the Taiping Civil War (1850-1864). The original basilica was completed in 1873. A second church built in 1935 was severely damaged by the Cultural Revolution. In 2007, Pope Benedict XVI established May 24 as a World Day of Prayer for the Church in China on the feast of Our Lady Help of Christians. It was under this title that Mary was originally invoked and venerated at the Sheshan retreat house that predated the basilica.

July 9	Chinese Martyrs (中華殉道聖人) or St. Augustine Zhao Rong and Companions	Honors 120 Catholics (87 Chinese and 33 Western missionaries consisting) martyred between 1648 (Qing Dynasty) and 1930 (Republic of China). Many died during the Boxer Rebellion of 1899-1901. They consisted of six bishops, twenty-three priests, one brother, seven sisters, seven seminarians, and seventy-six laypersons aged seven to seventy-nine years old. Augustine Zhao Rong was a bailiff in a local jail who was assigned to escort Catholic prisoners from Chengdu to Beijing during a 1772 persecution of Christians. Moved by their witness of faith and kindness during the 1500-mile journey he eventually asked to become a Christian. As a neophyte he evangelized other inquirers and was later ordained a diocesan priest in 1781 and served as a circuit rider. In a later anti-Catholic persecution in 1815, he was imprisoned and tortured, ultimately dying in jail from injuries he suffered at the hands of his former prison guard colleagues. The Chinese Martyrs were canonized by St. John Paul II in 2000.

Sept. 11	St. John Gabriel Perboyre, CM (董文學)	(1802-1840) French Vincentian priest, missionary in Henan and Hubei provinces of China. After a series of trials during which he refused to repudiate the faith, he was martyred by strangulation on a cross. Beatified in 1889. Canonized in 1996, the first saint in China to be canonized.
Nov. 8	Servant of God Xu Guangqi (徐光啓)	(1562-1633) Catholic convert from Shanghai, scholar-bureaucrat, scientist, mathematician, collaborator of Matteo Ricci during the Ming Dynasty. Considered one of the "Three Pillars of Chinese Catholicism." While not yet a blessed or saint, the Chinese faithful are encouraged to pray for his canonization. Nov. 8 is the anniversary of his death.

Bibliography

- Bays, Daniel H. *A New History of Christianity in China*. Malden, MA: Wiley-Blackwell. 2012.
- Catholic News Service. "Chinese priests ordered to put up signs banning children from churches." *www.catholicherald.co.uk/news/2018/02/09/chinese-priests-ordered-to-put-up-signs-banning-children-from-churches/*. Feb. 9, 2018. Accessed Apr. 27, 2018.
- Charbonnier, Jean-Pierre. *Christians in China: A.D. 600 to 2000*. San Francisco, CA: Ignatius Press. 2007.
- "Chinese Catholics to Celebrate the Tenth Anniversary of the Dedication of Our Lady of China Mosaic." Basilica of the National Shrine of the Immaculate Conception. Press Release. Aug. 4, 2012. *www.nationalshrine.com/atf/cf/%7BB0534716-4524-407D-A065-B68C4BFCB4BE%7D/OLO%20China%20Press%20Release.pdf*. Accessed Apr. 9, 2018.
- Jensen, Eric. "China Passes Mexico as Top Sending Country of Immigrants to the US." May 1, 2015, *www.census.gov/newsroom/blogs/research-matters/2015/05/china-replaces-mexico-as-the-top-sending-country-for-immigrants-to-the-united-states.html*. Accessed Apr. 9, 2018.
- Koetse, Manya. "China now has 33.5 million more men than women." Jan. 23, 2017, *www.whatsonweibo.com/china-now-335-million-men-women/*. Accessed Apr. 27, 2018.
- Kroeger, James H. "*Dialogue: Interpretive Key for the Life of the Church in Asia.*" FABC Papers no. 130. May 2010. *www.fabc.org/fabc%20papers/FABC%20paper%20130.pdf*. Accessed Apr. 27, 2018.

- Küng, Hans and Ching, Julia. *Christianity and Chinese Religions.* London: SCM Press. 1988.
- Lam, Anthony S.K. *The Catholic Church in Present-Day China: Through Darkness and Light.* Trans. Peter Barry, MM, and Norman Walling, SJ. Ed. Betty Ann Maheu and Anne Reusch. Hong Kong: Holy Spirit Study Centre; Leuven, Belgium: Ferdinand Verbiest Foundation. 1997.
- Livingston, Gretchen, and Anna Brown. "Intermarriage in the U.S. 50 Years after *Loving v. Virginia.*" May 18, 2017, *www.pewsocialtrends.org/2017/05/18/1-trends-and-patterns-in-intermarriage/.* Accessed Apr. 11, 2018.
- Mariscal, Jésus. "Evangelizing China." *Roman Echoes* 20(2). 2015.
- O'Malley, Vincent J. *Saints of Asia: 1500 to the Present.* Huntington, IN: Our Sunday Visitor. 2007.
- Park, Jerry Z., et al. "Asian Pacific Islander Catholics in the United States: A Preliminary Report." Jan. 2015, *www.usccb.org/issues-and-action/cultural-diversity/asian-pacific-islander/resources/upload/Asian-Pacific-Islander-Catholics-in-the-United-States-A-Preliminary-Report.pdf.* Accessed Apr. 9, 2018.
- Pope Benedict XVI, "Address of His Holiness Benedict XVI to Participants in the Pilgrimage Promoted by the Italian Dioceses of the Marche Region on the Occasion of the 400th Anniversary of the Death of Fr. Matteo Ricci," May 29, 2010, *www.vatican.va/content/benedict-xvi/en/speeches/2010/may/documents/hf_ben-xvi_spe_20100529_matteo-ricci.html.* Accessed Aug. 11, 2020.
- Pope John Paul II, "Message of Pope John Paul II to the Participants in the International Conference Commemorating

the Fourth Centenary of the Arrival in Beijing of Father Matteo Ricci," Oct. 24, 2001, *www.vatican.va/content/john-paul-ii/en/speeches/2001/october/documents/hf_jp-ii_spe_20011024_matteo-ricci.html*. Accessed Aug. 11, 2020.

- "Ryan, Joseph P. "American Contributions to the Catholic Missionary Effort in China in the Twentieth Century." *The Catholic Historical Review*, 31(2). 1945.
- Shavit, David. *The United States in Asia: A Historical Dictionary*. New York: Greenwood Press. 1990.
- USCCB Committee on Cultural Diversity in the Church Subcommittee on Asian and Pacific Island Affairs. *Harmony in Faith: Korean American Catholics*. Washington, DC: USCCB. 2014.
- USCCB Committee on Cultural Diversity in the Church Subcommittee on Asian and Pacific Island Affairs. *Resettling in Place: A Vietnamese American Catholic Experience*. Washington, DC: USCCB. 2014.
- USCCB. *Encountering Christ in Harmony: A Pastoral Response to Our Asian and Pacific Island Brothers and Sisters*. Washington, DC: USCCB. 2018.
- Yan, Kin Sheung C. *Evangelization in China*. New York: Orbis Books, 2014.
- Yee, Vivian, et al. "Here's the Reality About Illegal Immigrants in the United States." *The New York Times*, The New York Times, Mar. 6, 2017, *www.nytimes.com/interactive/2017/03/06/us/politics/undocumented-illegal-immigrants.html*. Accessed Apr. 9, 2018.
- Zavagnin, Anthony J. "Filling Empty Seats." *America: The Jesuit Review*, 215(14). Oct. 31, 2016.

Editorial Notes

In general, we have tried to use Pinyin system of romanization for Chinese names both for uniformity within this work and for the ease of the average contemporary reader for whom Pinyin is most likely the standard. In historical contexts where this may result in confusion or difficulty, especially with respect to historical source material, we have also included the then-current romanizations. One risk of this approach is that we might have used a romanization that the actual persons involved may not have preferred; no disrespect is intended by this choice.

Chinese convention places the family name first whereas American English convention places the family name last. Names in this book follow both conventions, where Chinese names without any English follow the Chinese convention (e.g., Xu Guangqi, where Xu is the family name, and Guangqi is the given name) and names of Chinese Americans with English given names follow the American English convention (e.g., Fr. Paul Pang, where Pang is the family name). Some persons are named with a combination of both Chinese and English names. In these cases the surname is usually the first romanized Chinese word (e.g., Cardinal Thomas Tian Gengxin, where Tian is the family name, Thomas is the English given name, and Gengxin is the Chinese given name).